ŠEVČÍK
Op. 2 Part 1

SCHOOL OF BOWING TECHNIQUE

SCHULE DER BOGENTECHNIK

ÉCOLE DU MÉCANISME DE L'ARCH

for

VIOLA
(ALTO)

arranged / bearbeitet / arrangées

by   von   par

Lionel Tertis

Italian viola by Pietro Giovanni Mantegazza, c. 1780,
with kind permission of Christie's, London.

Bosworth

ABRÉVIATIONS ET SIGNES	ABREVIATIONS AND EXPLANATIONS	ABKÜRZUNGEN UND ZEICHEN
W = Tout l'archet	W = Whole length of bow	W = Ganzer Bogen
H = Moitié de l'archet	H = Half length of bow	H = Halber Bogen
L H = Moitié inférieure	L H = Lower half of bow	L H = Untere Hälfte des Bogens
U H = Moitié supérieure	U H = Upper half of bow	U H = Obere Hälfte des Bogens
⅓ B = Un tiers de l'archet	⅓ B = Third of bow	⅓ B = Ein Drittel des Bogens
N = Talon de l'archet	N = Nut-end (Heel of bow)	N = Am Frosch des Bogens
M = Milieu de l'archet	M = Middle of bow	M = Mitte des Bogens
P = Pointe de l'archet	P = Point of bow	P = Spitze des Bogens
M* = Travailler de trois façons: (1) du milieu de l'archet (2) de la pointe de l'archet (3) du talon de l'archet	M* = Practise in three ways: (1) in middle of bow (2) at the point (3) at the heel	M* = Übe in drei Arten: (1) mit der Mitte des Bogens (2) mit der Spitze des Bogens (3) am Frosch des Bogens
⊓ = Tirez	⊓ = Down bow	⊓ = Abstrich
V = Poussez	V = Up bow	V = Aufstrich
— = Soutenu. Tiré large, avec peu d'interruption entre les notes, particulièrement entre deux et plusieurs notes sur un archet.	— = Well sustained - may also be interpreted as broad and sustained with slight detachment between notes, especially with two or more notes in same bow.	— = Gehalten. Wird breit gezogen, mit geringen Trennungen zwischen den Noten gespielt, besonders bei zwei und mehr Noten auf einem Bogen.
• = Staccato. Travailler séparément avec beaucoup et peu d'archet et, jouer court; laisser l'archet sur la corde lorsqu'il y a 2 ou plusieurs notes à l'archet.	• = Staccato i.e., Articulating each note separately and short, whether short or long bows, or articulating two or more notes in same bow with bow on string.	• = Staccato. Sowohl mit viel als wenig Bogen getrennt und kurz zu spielen; bei zwei und mehr Noten auf einem Bogen bleibt der Bogen auf der Saite.
Ma = Martelé. Coups d'archet detachés accentués, en laissant l'archet sur la corde.	Ma = Martelé i.e., detached accentuated separate bows with bow on string.	Ma = Martelé. Getrennte, akzentuierte Bogenstriche, wobei der Bogen auf der Saite bleibt.
Sa = Sautillé. Archet jeté ou sautillé avec deux ou plusieurs notes à l'archet.	Sa = Sautillé i.e., springing or bounding bow with two or more notes in same bow.	Sa = Sautillé. Springender oder geworfener Strich mit zwei oder mehr Noten auf einem Bogen.
⋏ = Spiccato Très peu d'archet, en levant l'archet de la corde après chaque note.	⋏ = Spiccato i.e. extremely short bow with bow off the string after each note.	⋏ = Spiccato. Sehr kurze Striche, wobei der Bogen nach jeder Note von der Saite gehoben wird.
) = Lever l'archet de la corde.	) = Bow to be raised from the string.	) = Bogen von der Saite heben.
Legato. Liaison souple de note à note avec pression régulière de l'archet ou en pressions variées.	Legato, i.e. smoothly or well-bound from one note to another—with even pressure of bow whether played forte or piano or with various shades of expression.	Legato. Geschmeidige Bindung von Note zu Note mit gleichmässigem Bogendruck oder in verschiedenen Stärkegraden.
* = A défaut de ce signe au début d'un exercice, commencer par le tiré au talon.	* = If there is no sign at the beginning of an exercise, begin the first note at the heel with a down bow.	* = Wenn dieses Zeichen nicht am Anfang einer Übung steht, beginnt sie immer am Frosch im Abstrich.

B. & Co. Ltd. 21692

1

EXERCICES PRÉPARATOIRES	PREPARATORY EXERCISES	VORBEREITENDE ÜBUNGEN
Jouez le No. 1 avec de petits coups d'archet *a)* au milieu *b)* à la pointe *c)* au talon. Pendant les repos, l'archet doit rester constamment maintenu sur la corde sans le moindre son cependant que ces repos sont rigoureusement comptés.	Practise No. 1 with very little bow *a)* in the middle *b)* at the point *c)* at the heel. During the rests, the bow must remain on the string without the slightest sound while the rests are strictly counted.	Übe Nr. 1 mit sehr wenig Bogen *a)* in der Mitte *b)* an der Spitze *c)* am Frosch. Während der Pausen muß der Bogen ohne jeden Ton auf der Saite ruhen, während die Pausen genau ausgezählt werden.

2

Jouez les **18** exemples ci-après selon les six manières suivantes sans ôter l'archet.	Play the **18** examples below without raising the bow in the following VI styles.	Übe die untenstehenden **18** Beispiele ohne den Bogen abzuheben in den folgenden **6** Arten.

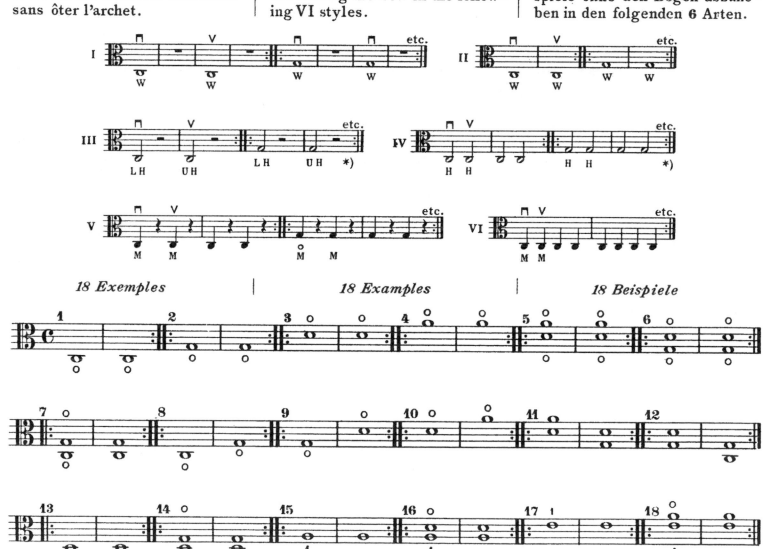

18 Exemples	*18 Examples*	*18 Beispiele*

* D'abord avec la moitié inférieure ensuite avec la moitié supérieure de l'archet. (L'archet ne quitte pas la corde pendant les repos).	* First with the lower and then with the upper half of the bow. (Bow on string during rests.)	* Zuerst mit der unteren, dann mit der oberen Hälfte des Bogens. (Der Bogen bleibt in den Pausen auf der Saite liegen.)

Copyright 1956 by Bosworth & Co. Ltd.

Propriété pour la France et la Belgique, Bosworth & Co., Bruxelles

B.& Co.Ltd. 21692a

Made in England
Imprimé en Angleterre

3

Jouez tout l'exercice selon les différents exemples indiqués. | Practise each example throughout the whole exercise. | Diese Übung ist in allen angegebenen Varianten zu spielen.

Sostenuto *(Sustained)*

57 Exemples
Pendant les repos l'archet est maintenu sur la corde sans le moindre son. | *57 Examples*
Bow must remain on string during rests without slightest sound. | *57 Beispiele*
Der Bogen muß während der Pausen ohne jeden Ton auf der Saite ruhen.

) Lever l'archet
) Raise bow from string
) Bogen von der Saite abheben

D'arbord avec la moitié inférieure ensuite, avec la moitié supérieure de l'archet.

First with the lower, then with the upper half of the bow.

Erst mit der unteren, dann mit der oberen Hälfte des Bogens.

4

Jouez tout cet exercice selon les différents exemples indiqués.

Each example to be practised throughout the whole exercise.

Diese Übung ist in allen angegebenen Varianten zu spielen.

Andante

75 Exemples | 75 Examples | 75 Beispiele

1er temps avec l'inférieure, 2e temps avec la moitié superieure de l'archet.

1st time with lower 2nd time with upper, half of bow.

Das erste Mal mit der unteren, das zweite Mal mit der oberen Hälfte des Bogens.

* Même indication de métronome:- Exemples 8 à 14

* Same metronome mark:- Examples 8 to 14

* Dasselbe Metronom-Zeichen: Beispiele 8-14

B.& Co.Ltd.21692ª

8

Maintenez l'archet sur la corde
pendant les repos.

Bow on string during rests.

Der Bogen ruht auf der Saite
während der Pausen.

5

Jouez également cet exercice dans la 6e position (Voir exercice No. 8) dans **260** exemples de coups d'archet.

Practise this exercise also in the 6th position (see exercise No. 8) in the **260** examples of bowing.

Spiele diese Übung auch in der 6. Lage (siehe Übung Nr. 8) in den **260** Beispielen verschiedener Stricharten.

Moderato

2e Viola   2nd Viola   2.Viola

260 différents exemples de coups d'archet.

260 examples in various bowings.

260 Beispiele in verschiedenen Stricharten.

Jeu du poignet. Use your wrist. Mit dem Handgelenk.

12

14

Lever l'archet après chaque note détachée. | Bow off after each staccato note. | Nach jeder Staccato-Note Bogen abheben.

Avec très peu d'archet. | Very little bow. | Mit sehr wenig Bogen.

B. & Co. Ltd. 21692ᵃ

6

Exercice avec 214 exemples de coups d'archet.	*Exercise with 214 examples of bowing.*	*Übe in 214 Beispielen verschiedener Stricharten.*
Jouez également cet exercice dans la 7e position (Voir exercice No. 10) dans les différents exemples de coups d'archet.	Practise this exercise also in the 7th position (see exercise No.10) in the various examples of bowing.	Spiele diese Übung auch in der 7. Lage (siehe Übung Nr. 10) in den verschiedenen Stricharten.

Allegro moderato

214 différents exemples de coups d'archet.	*214 examples of various bowings.*	*214 Beispiele verschiedener Stricharten.*

B.& Co. Ltd.21692ᵃ

16

Jeu du poignet. | Use your wrist. | Mit dem Handgelenk.

B.& Co.Ltd.21692a

Tous les coups d'archet de **203, 204, 205 et 206** avec la pointe de l'archet.

All bowings of **203, 204, 205, 206** at the point of bow.

Alle Bogenstriche von **203, 204, 205, 206** an der Spitze des Bogens.

7

Chacun de ces **91** exemples doit être successivement appliqué à tout l'exercice. Jouez également cet exercice dans la **5e** position (Voir No. 9) dans les différents coups d'archet.

Each of the **91** examples to be practised throughout the whole exercise. To be also practised in the **5th** position (see No. 9) in the various bowings.

Die ganze Übung ist in **91** Varianten zu spielen - ebenso in der **5.** Lage (siehe Übung Nr. 9) in den verschiedenen Stricharten.

Allegretto

91 exemples différents de coups d'archet.

91 examples in various bowings.

91 Beispiele in den verschiedenen Stricharten.

Jeu du poignet. | Use your wrist. | Mit dem Handgelenk.

8

Voir exercice No. 5 | See exercise No. 5 | Siehe Übung Nr. 5

9

Voir exercice No. 7 | See exercise No. 7 | Siehe Übung Nr. 7

10

Voir exercice No. 6 | See exercise No. 6 | Siehe Übung Nr. 6

11

Jouez cet exercice d'après les exemples (1 à 198) du No. 6.

Practise this exercise in the examples (1 to 198) of No. 6.

Spiele diese Übung in den Varianten (1-198) von Nr. 6

12

Jouez cet exercice d'après les exemples (1 à 198) du No. 6.

Practise this exercise in the examples (1 to 198) of No. 6.

Spiele diese Übung in den Varianten (1-198) von Nr. 6

B.& Co. Ltd. 21692ª

13

L'exercice No. 13 doit être joué, chaque fois en son entier, selon les 105 différents exemples de coups d'archet qui suivent, tout en veillant à n'employer que les parties de l'archet comme l'indiquent les divers signes et abréviations. On agira de la même façon pour l'exercice No. 26 que l'on jouera dans la 7e position.

Exercise No. 13 to be practised throughout in the following 105 examples of bowing, taking care to use only the various parts of the bow as indicated by the signs and abbreviations the same procedure to be applied to exercise No. 26 in the 7th position.

Die ganze Übung Nr. 13 ist in den folgenden 105 Bogenstricharten zu spielen, wobei zu beachten ist, daß nur die Teile des Bogens zu gebrauchen sind, die durch Zeichen und Abkürzungen angedeutet sind. Dasselbe gilt für die Übung Nr. 26 in der 7. Lage.

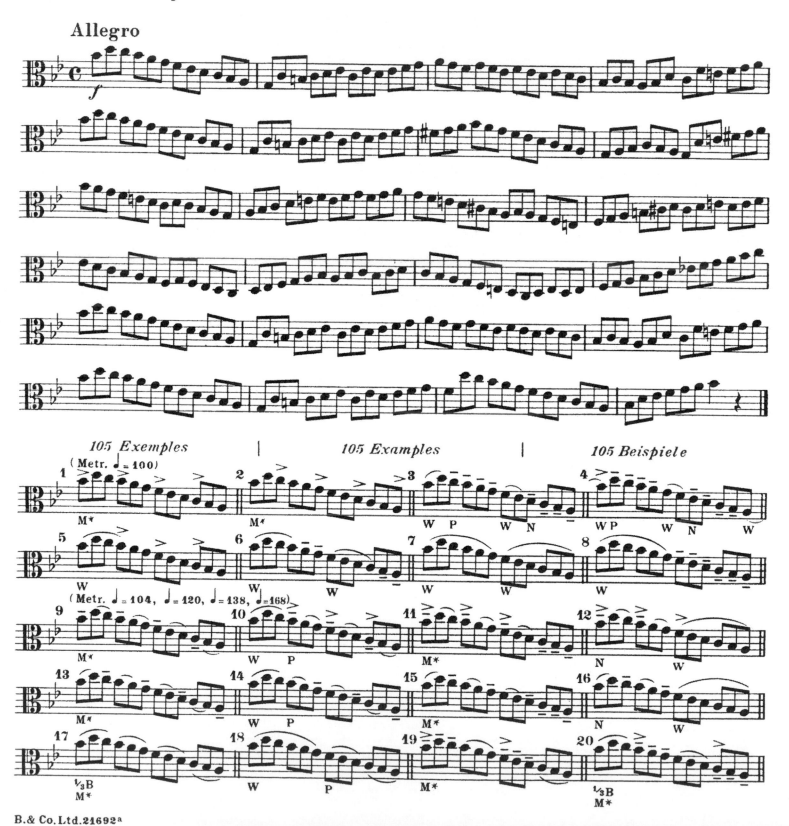

B.& Co. Ltd. 21692a

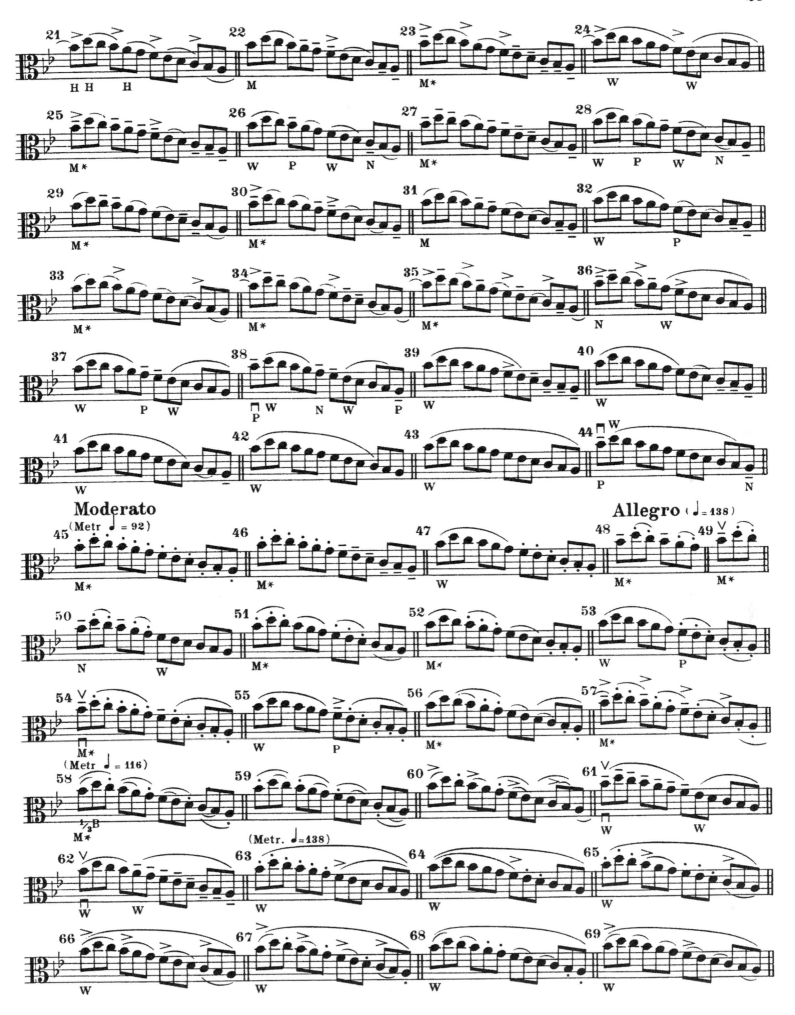

In examples **98** to **105**, don't amplify or soften suddenly or spasmodically. Your tone should swell or decrease from *p* to *f* or *f* to *p* gradually.

14

L'exercice No.14 avec 77 exemples de coups d'archet, également d'application pour l'exercice No. 25 dans la 4e position.

Exercise No.14 with 77 examples of bowing which also apply to Exercise No. 25 in the 4th position.

Übung Nr.14 mit 77 Beispielen verschiedener Stricharten, die auch für die Übung No. 25 in der 4. Lage zutreffen.

15

L'exercice No. 15 avec 64 exemples de coups d'archet, également applicable à l'exercice No.27 dans la 4e position.

Exercise No.15 with 64 examples of bowing which also apply to Exercise No.27 in the 4th position.

Übung Nr. 15 mit 64 Beispielen verschiedener Stricharten, die auch für die Übung No. 27 in der 4. Lage zutreffen.

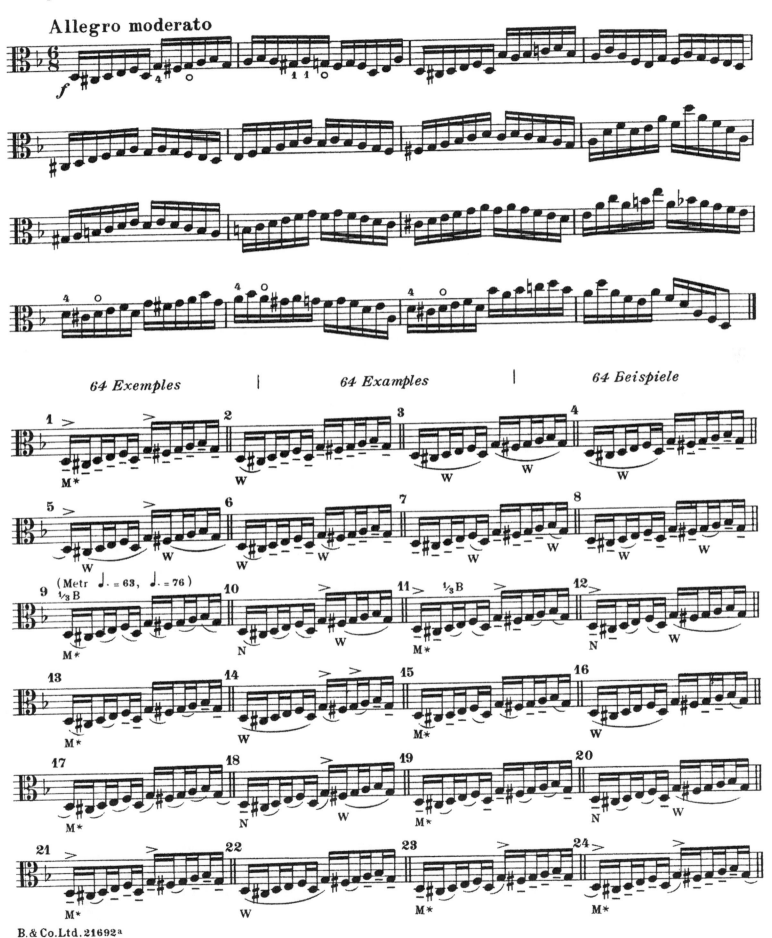

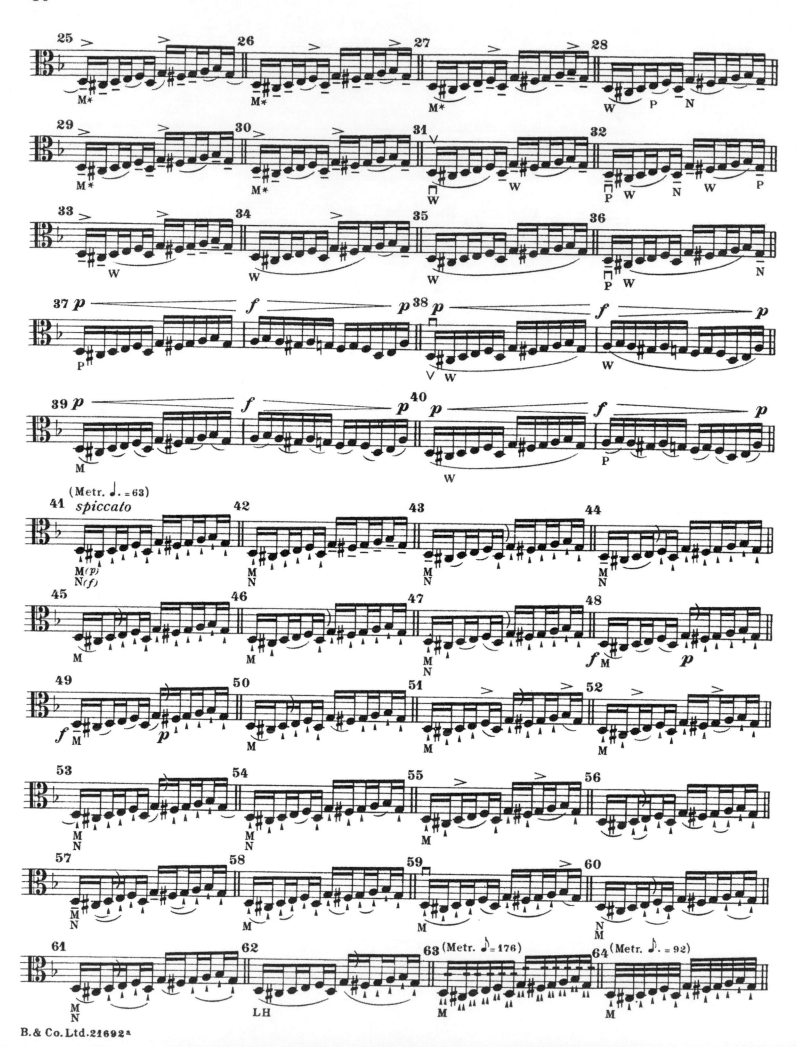

16

Exercice No.16 avec 68 exemples
de coups d'archet.

Exercise No.16 with 68 examples
of bowing.

Übung Nr. 16 mit 68 Beispielen
verschiedener Stricharten.

Allegro moderato

68 Exemples | 68 Examples | 68 Beispiele

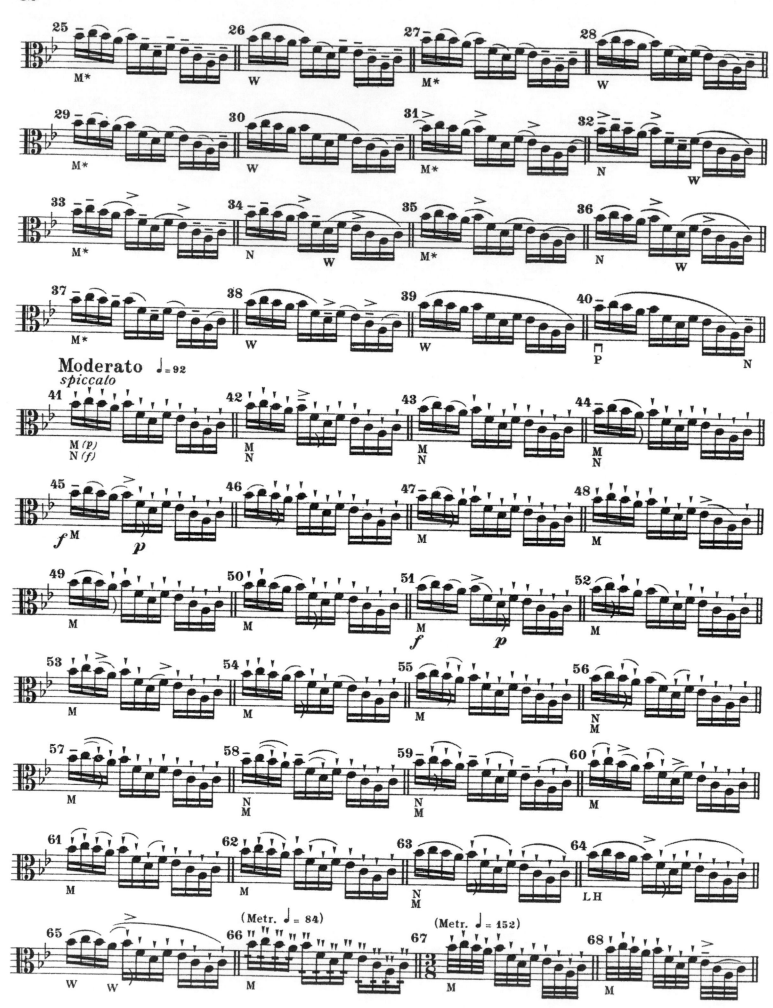

17

L'exercice No.17 avec 131 exemples de coups d'archet, également d'application pour l'exercice No. 28 dans la 5e position. | Exercise No. 17 with 131 examples of bowing which also apply to Exercise No. 28 in the 5th position. | Übung Nr. 17 mit 131 Beispielen verschiedener Stricharten, die auch für die Übung No. 28 in der 5. Lage zutreffen.

Allegro

131 Exemples | 131 Examples | 131 Beispiele

S'il n'y a qu'un quart ou une demie barre de mesure indiquée la deuxième partie de la mesure se joue avec le même coup d'archet que la première partie. | Where only a quarter or a half bar is given, the second half of the bar to be bowed exactly like the first. | Wo nur ein viertel oder halber Takt angegeben ist, muß der zweite Teil des Taktes genau so gespielt werden wie der erste.

B.& Co. Ltd. 21692ᵃ

34

B.& Co.Ltd. 21692a

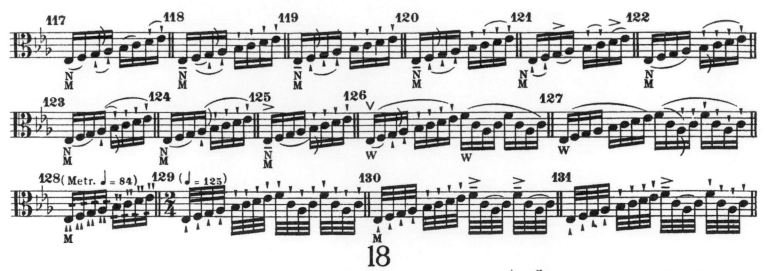

18

Exercice No.18 à jouer Pianissimo avec 30 exemples.
Ces exercices doivent être joués "flautando" c. à d. que l'archet doit être tiré aussi légèrement que possible et vers l'extrémité du manche.

Exercise No.18 for Pianissimo playing with 30 examples.
These exercises to be also practised "flautando" i.e., bow to be drawn as lightly as possible over the end of the fingerboard.

Übung Nr.18 zum Studium des Pianissimo - Spiels mit 30 Beispielen.
Diese Übungen werden auch "flautando" geübt, d.h. der Bogen wird so leicht wie möglich über das Ende des Griffbrettes gezogen.

19

Continuation de l'exercice pianissi-mo comme Exercice No.18. | Continuation of exercises in **pp** playing as in Exercise No. 18 | Nr. 19 Fortsetzung der Pianissi-mo - Übung, wie in Übung Nr. 18

Moderato ♩ = 80

59 Exemples | *59 Examples* | *59 Beispiele*

B. & Co. Ltd. 21692ᵃ

38

B.& Co. Ltd. 21692ᵃ

20

L'exercice No. 20 vise à vous faire acquérir un emploi parcimonieux de l'archet qu'il soit tiré sur les cordes en *f* ou en *p*. Appliquez successivement chacun des exemples qui suivent à tout l'exercice comme indiqué par le No. de la page. - Chaque exercice doit être joué en son entier des trois façons suivantes:-

a) 2 mesures par archet complet.
b) 4 mesures par archet complet.
c) 8 mesures par archet complet.

Exercise No. 20 for cultivating extreme economy in the use of the bow whether drawn across the strings forte or piano.
Practise each of the following examples throughout entire exercise (as indicated by the number of page). Each exercise to be practised:-

a) 2 bars to a full length bow.
b) 4 bars to a full length bow.
c) 8 bars to a full length bow.

Übung Nr. 20 - Zur Erlernung der äussersten Sparsamkeit in der Bogeneinteilung, gleichviel ob forte oder piano. Spiele die ganze Übung in den folgenden Varianten wie aus den angegebenen Seitenzahlen ersichtlich ist. Jede Übung ist zu spielen:

a) 2 Takte auf einem ganzen Bogen.
b) 4 Takte auf einem ganzen Bogen.
c) 8 Takte auf einem ganzen Bogen.

Voir les exercices No. 3 (Page 5) | *See exercise No. 3 (Page 5)* | *Siehe Übung Nr. 3 (Seite 5)*

Voir les exercices No. 4 (Page 7) | *See exercise No. 4 (Page 7)* | *Siehe Übung Nr. 4 (Seite 7)*

Voir les exercices No. 5 (Page 9) | *See exercise No. 5 (Page 9)* | *Siehe Übung Nr. 5 (Seite 9)*

Voir les exercices No. 7 (Page 20) | *See exercise No. 7 (Page 20)* | *Siehe Übung Nr. 7 (Seite 20)*

Voir les exercices No. 6 (Page 15) | *See exercise No. 6 (Page 15)* | *Siehe Übung Nr. 6 (Seite 15)*

Voir les exercices No. 14 (Page 27) | *See exercise No. 14 (Page 27)* | *Siehe Übung Nr. 14 (Seite 27)*

40

21

Exercice No. 21 (No. 22, No. 23, No. 24) avec coup d'archet glissant sur les différentes cordes.
Les coups d'archet à employer pour le No. 21 sont: exemples 1 à 97 de l'exercice No. 13.

Exercises No. 21, (No. 22, No. 23 and No. 24) for bowing across the strings.
The bowings to be used for No. 21 are:- Examples 1 to 97 of exercise No. 13.

Die Übungen Nr. 21, 22, 23 und 24 dienen zur Erlernung des Bogenstriches.
Folgende Bogenstricharten werden für Übung Nr. 21 benutzt. Beispiele 1 - 97 der Übung Nr. 13.

22

Avec les coups d'archet des exemples de l'exercice No. 16.

With the bowings shown in the examples of exercise No. 16.

Mit den Stricharten der Beispiele der Übung Nr. 16.

B. & Co. Ltd. 21692ª

23

Avec les coups d'archet des exemples de l'exercice No. 17. | With the bowings shown in the examples of exercise No. 17. | Mit den Stricharten der Beispiele der Übung Nr. 17.

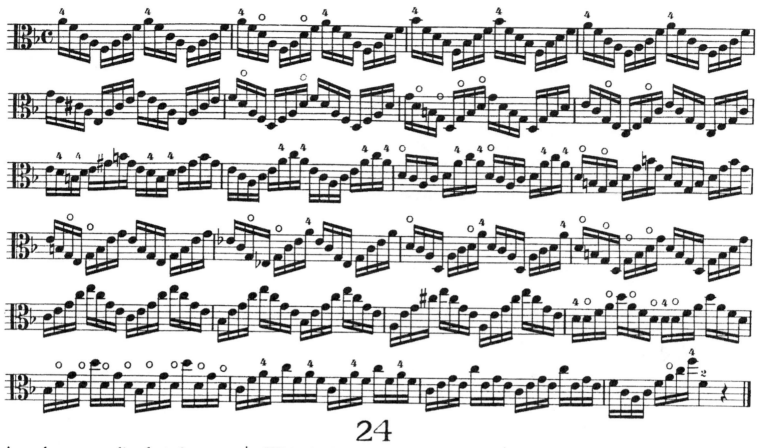

24

Avec les coups d'archet des exemples de l'exercice No. 15. | With the bowings shown in the examples of exercise No. 15. | Mit den Stricharten der Beispiele der Übung Nr. 15.

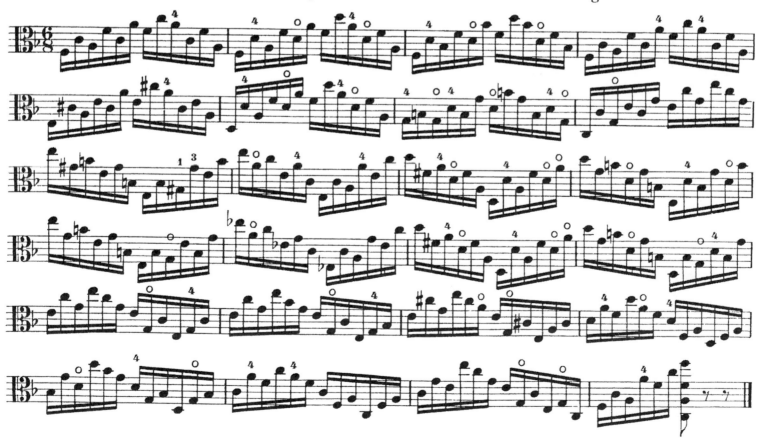

B.& Co. Ltd. 21692ª

25

Exercice No.25 (No. 26, No.27 et No.28) en position plus élevée avec les coups d'archet des exemples de l'exercice No.14.

Exercise No.25 (No. 26, No.27 and No.28) in higher positions with the bowings shown in the examples of exercise No.14.

Die Übungen Nr. 25, 26, 27 und 28 in höheren Lagen mit den Stricharten der Beispiele der Übung Nr. 14.

26

Avec les coups d'archet des exemples de l'exercice No.13.

With the bowings shown in the examples of exercise No.13.

Mit den Stricharten der Beispiele der Übung Nr. 13.

27

| Avec les coups d'archet des ex- emples de l'exercice No. 15. | With the bowings shown in the examples of exercise No. 15. | Mit den Stricharten der Beispiele der Übung Nr. 15. |

28

| Avec les coups d'archet des ex- emples de l'exercice No. 17. | With the bowings shown in the examples of exercise No. 17. | Mit den Stricharten der Beispiele der Übung Nr. 17. |

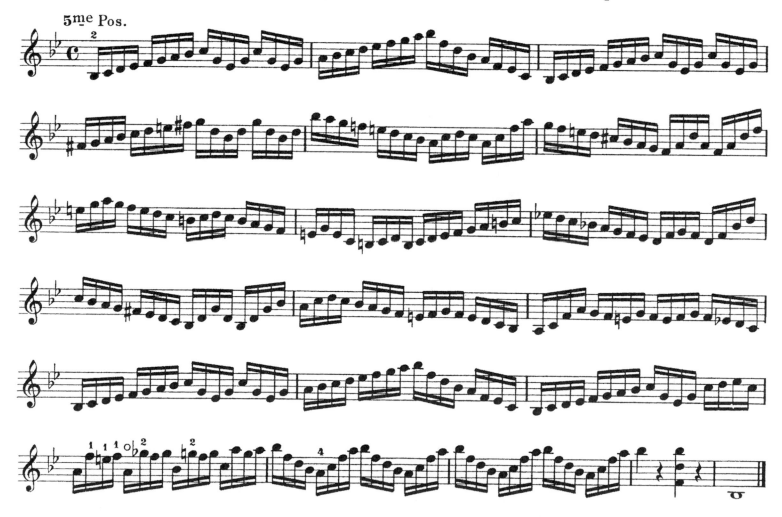

B.& Co.Ltd.21692ᵃ